Guess What!

Activity Book 4

with Online Resources

British English

Lynne Marie Robertson

Series Editor: Lesley Koustaff

CAMBRIDGE UNIVERSITY PRESS

Shaftesbury Road, Cambridge CB2 8EA, United Kingdom

One Liberty Plaza, 20th Floor, New York, NY 10006, USA

477 Williamstown Road, Port Melbourne, VIC 3207, Australia

314–321, 3rd Floor, Plot 3, Splendor Forum, Jasola District Centre, New Delhi – 110025, India

103 Penang Road, #05-06/07, Visioncrest Commercial, Singapore 238467

Cambridge University Press & Assessment is a department of the University of Cambridge.

We share the University's mission to contribute to society through the pursuit of education, learning and research at the highest international levels of excellence.

www.cambridge.org
Information on this title: www.cambridge.org/9781107545380

First published 2016

40 39 38 37 36 35 34 33 32

Printed in Malaysia by Vivar Printing

A catalogue record for this publication is available from the British Library

ISBN 978-1-107-54538-0 Activity Book with Online Resources Level 4
ISBN 978-1-107-54535-9 Pupil's Book Level 4
ISBN 978-1-107-55607-2 Teacher's Book with DVD Level 4
ISBN 978-1-107-54544-1 Class Audio CDs Level 4
ISBN 978-1-107-54546-5 Flashcards Level 4
ISBN 978-1-107-54548-9 Presentation Plus DVD-ROM Level 4
ISBN 978-1-107-52826-0 Teacher's Resource and Tests CD-ROM Levels 3–4

Additional resources for this publication at www.cambridge.org/guesswhat

Contents

Welcome back!

1 **Look and write the number.**

□	□	□	□	□	1
curly hair	straight hair	fair hair	red hair	dark hair	glasses

2 **Look and write the words.**

1 He's got _____ *short* _____ hair.

2 He's got _____ hair.

3 He's got _____ hair.

4 He's got _____ .

5 She's got _____ *long* _____ hair.

6 She's got _____ .

7 She's got _____ hair.

8 She's got _____ hair.

3 **Think** **Look at activity 2. Write the words.**

How are they the same?	How are they different?

1 He's got _____ *curly* _____ hair.
   She's got _____ *curly* _____ hair.
2 He's got _____ .
   She's got _____ .
	3 He's got _____ hair.
	   She's got _____ hair.
	4 He's got _____ hair.
	   She's got _____ hair.

My picture dictionary → Go to page 84: Find and write the new words.

4 Read and match.

1 She's tall. She's got short straight hair. _____b____

2 He's short. He's got big glasses. _____

3 She's tall. She's got long straight hair. _____

4 He's short. He's got small glasses. _____

5 She's short. She's got curly red hair. _____

5 Look and complete the questions and answers.

1 (Tim) What does _____he look like?_____

_____ tall. _____

short fair hair and big glasses.

2 (Helen) What does _____?

_____ short. _____

short curly hair and small glasses.

3 (Simon) What does _____?

_____ short. _____

curly dark hair and small sunglasses.

4 (Laura) What does _____?

_____ tall. _____ straight red hair and big sunglasses.

Tim   Helen   Simon   Laura

6 Write about a person in your family.

My ... has got ... hair _____

_____

_____

Look and match. Then write the answers.

| 86 cm | ~~1 m 23 cm~~ | 28 cm | 1 m 55 cm | 64 cm |

1 How tall is the boy?   He's 1 metre 23 centimetres.

2 How high is the chair?   It's _____

3 How tall is the girl?   _____

4 How tall is the rabbit?   _____

5 How high is the guitar?   _____

8 Answer the questions.

1 How tall is your friend?   _____

2 How tall is your mum/dad?   _____

3 How tall are you?   _____

4 How high is your chair?   _____

Skills: *Writing*

9 **Read the paragraph and write the words.**

> dark   short   ~~1 m 22 cm~~   cinema   blue   playing   71 cm   bike

My friend's name is Paul. He's ¹ __1 m 22 cm__ tall.

He's got ² _____ ³ _____ hair.

He likes ⁴ _____ football. He's got a

⁵ _____ ⁶ _____ . It's ⁷ _____ high.

He likes going to the ⁸ _____ on Saturdays.

10 **(About Me) Answer the questions.**

1 What's your friend's name?

My friend's name is _____

2 How tall is your friend?

_____

3 What does your friend look like?

_____

4 What sports does your friend like?

_____

5 What activities does your friend like doing?

_____

11 **(About Me) Write about your friend.**

My friend's _____

_____

_____

12 **(About Me) Think of a friend. Ask and answer with another friend.**

> What does your friend look like?   She's got fair hair and glasses.

> Is it Mary?   Yes, it is!

13 **Read and match.**

> **1** Let's register now!   **3** We all like adventures.
> **2** ~~No, let's watch TV.~~   **4** Do you want to help your local community?

a

What shall we do this afternoon?

How about swimming?

_____ 2

b

I do! I do!

Anna! Sit down.

c

We're making a new adventure playground. Register online for the free app.

How exciting! _____

d

What shall we call our team?

How about the Adventurers? _____ .

Good idea.

14 **Look at activity 13. Circle the answers.**

1 They want to _____ .
   a play in the rain   **b** go swimming   **c** (watch TV)

2 *Daisy does it!* is the name of _____ .
   a their friend   **b** their community   **c** a TV programme

3 The TV programme asks them to _____ .
   a make a new supermarket   **b** help their community
   c make a new school

4 They register to _____ .
   a get a free app   **b** watch TV   **c** sit down

5 The Adventurers is the name of _____ .
   a their team   **b** the local community   **c** the new playground

15 Read and tick the activities that show the value: get involved with your local community.

1 help make a playground ✓

2 ride your bike ☐

3 pick up litter ☐

4 go to school ☐

5 read a book ☐

6 clean the beach ☐

16 Find and tick the words that sound like *owl*.

1

 a ✓

 b ✓

 c ☐

2

 a ☐

 b ☐

 c ☐

3

 a ☐

 b ☐

 c ☐

4

 a ☐

 b ☐

 c ☐

What **patterns** can you see?

1 Look and read. Circle the patterns you can see.

1 zigzags and wavy lines
(wavy lines and stripes)
stripes and zigzags

2 spots and stripes
wavy lines and spots
zigzags and spots

3 wavy lines and stripes
stripes and zigzags
zigzags and wavy lines

2 Read and draw.

1
Draw four green zigzags at the top.
Draw six red stripes under the zigzags.
Draw two purple spots under the stripes.

2
Draw a circle.
Draw nine blue spots in the circle.
Draw three orange stripes next to the circle.

3
Draw a big square.
Draw seven yellow stripes in the square.
Draw six black wavy lines between the stripes.

Evaluation

1 **Look and write the questions and answers. Then match.**

1 What does Sally
look _like_ ? ←

2 What does Herman
_____ _____ ?

3 What does Macy
_____ _____ ?

4 What does Raul
_____ _____ ?

Raul

Sally

Herman

Macy

a _____ tall. _____
_____ fair hair and
sunglasses.

b _____ short. _____
_____ long straight
hair and small glasses.

c _She's_ tall. _She's_
got curly red hair
and sunglasses.

d _____ short. _____
_____ short dark hair
and big glasses.

2 (About Me) **Complete the sentences about this unit.**

1 I can talk about _____ .

2 I can write about _____ .

3 My favourite part is _____ .

3 (Puzzle) **Guess what it is.**

Hair that's not straight.
What is it? _____

Go to page 93 and write the answer.

11

1 Fun sports

1 **Look and write the numbers.**

| | mountain biking | | snowboarding | 1 | sailing | | fishing | | skiing |

| | ice skating | | bowling | | kayaking | | skateboarding |

2 **Think** **Where do you do the sports? Look at activity 1 and write.**

river/sea	mountain	city/town
1 _sailing_	4 _____	7 _____
2 _____	5 _____	8 _____
3 _____	6 _____	9 _____

My picture dictionary ➔ Go to page 85: Find and write the new words.

3 **Look and read. Then circle.**

1 **He's / He isn't** very good at kayaking.
2 **She's / She isn't** good at mountain biking.
3 **He's / He isn't** good at skateboarding.

4 **He's / He isn't** very good at ice skating.
5 **She's / She isn't** good at skiing.

4 **Look and write the words.**

I'm not very good at _skateboarding_ .

_____ good at ice skating.

_____ very good at _____ .

_____

5 Complete the conversations.

1 Are you _good at bowling?_
Yes, _I am_ .

2 _____ good
at ice skating?
No, _____ .

3 _____
good at?
_____ good at playing
the piano.

6 Think Look and write.

Ben	mountain biking ✗	guitar ✓	Liz	kayaking ✓	violin ✗

1 **Ben:** _Are you_ good at playing the violin? **Liz:** _No, I'm not._

2 **Liz:** _____ good at mountain biking?

   Ben: _____

3 **Ben:** _____ good at?

   Liz: _____ good at _____ .

4 **Liz:** _____ good at?

   Ben: _____ good at _____ .

7 About Me Answer the questions.

1 Are you good at music? _____

2 Are you good at skiing? _____

3 What are you good at? _____

4 What are you not very good at? _____

5 What do you want to be good at? _____

Skills: *Writing*

8 (About Me) **Read and answer. Circle *yes* or *no*.**

Are you good at … ?

Music	yes	no	making films	yes	no
Art	yes	no	playing table tennis	yes	no
dancing	yes	no	gymnastics	yes	no
singing	yes	no	karate	yes	no
playing the piano	yes	no	playing the guitar	yes	no

9 **Ask three friends. Write their name and answers.**

What are you good at?   I'm good at singing.

Name:	Good at:

10 **Look at activities 8 and 9. Plan a talent show.**

Talent show!

Time: 6 o'clock
Place: gym

1 Heidi's good at singing. And she can dance.

2 Jim's good at playing the guitar.

3 Me – I'm good at making films about karate.

Talent show!

Time: _____

Place: _____

1 _____
_____

2 _____
_____

3 _____
_____

11 Read and number in order.

a — Who wants to help paint the wall?

I do! I'm good at painting.

So are we, Anna! Let's all help.

b — It looks great. Well done!

It's me!

c — Wait and see, Anna.

Who are you painting, Lily?

d — Red hair and green eyes. Good!

Can I see?

Shh, Anna!

e — Welcome to Pinton Woods! I'm Daisy.

Hello. We're the Adventurers.

f — Thanks, Grandma!

We don't need this paint. Here you are.

1

12 Look at activity 11. Answer the questions.

1 Who gives paint to the children? *Grandma.*

2 What do the children help to paint?

3 Are the children good at painting?

4 Who does Lily paint?

5 Does Daisy like the wall painting?

13 Look and tick the picture that shows the value: allow others to work.

1

2

3

14 Find and tick the words that sound like *coil*.

1 **a**

b

c

2 **a**

b

c

3 **a**

b

c

What type of body movements can we make?

1 What body movements can you see? Circle the correct words.

1 stretch, bend, kick
~~kick, bend, stretch~~
(bend, stretch, kick)

2 turn, stretch, shake
shake, stretch, turn
bend, stretch, turn

3 shake, bend, kick
kick, shake, turn
shake, turn, bend

2 Complete the sentences with body movements.

1 She can _b e n d_ her body.

2 He can _ _ _ _ his head.

3 She wants to _ _ _ _ _ _ _ her legs.

4 Let's _ _ _ _ _ the musical instruments.

5 He can _ _ _ _ the ball.

Evaluation

1 **Look and write.**

1

What are you good at?

___I'm good___ at making models.

2

What are you good at?

_____ good at skiing.

3

_____

_____

4

_____

_____

5

_____

_____

2 **(About Me) Complete the sentences about this unit.**

1 I can talk about _____ .

2 I can write about _____ .

3 My favourite part is _____ .

3 **Puzzle Guess what it is.**

You need water and wind to do this sport. What is it? _____

Go to page 93 and write the answer.

2 Around town

1 Look and number the picture.

1 ~~shopping centre~~
2 underground station
3 bus station
4 restaurant
5 square
6 bank

2 Think Read and match. Then write the words.

1 It means *stop* and *go*. It's red, yellow, and green.
2 It's black and white. It's not an animal.
3 I can eat here.
4 I can sleep here.
5 I can see art here.

museum
restaurant
~~traffic light~~
hotel
zebra crossing

_____ _____ *traffic light* _____ _____

My picture dictionary Go to page 86: Find and write the new words.

3 Look and circle the correct answers.

1 Where's the restaurant?
It's . . . . the hotel.
a (above)   b opposite   c below

2 Where's the museum?
It's . . . . the traffic light.
a below   b opposite   c far from

3 Where's the underground station?
It's . . . . the hotel.
a below   b next to   c above

4 Where's the shopping centre?
It's . . . . the museum.
a opposite   b next to   c far from

5 Where's the bank?
It's . . . . the zebra crossing.
a near   b below   c far from

 Look at activity 3. Complete the questions and answers.

1 _Where's_ the train?

It's _next to_ the hotel.

2 _____ the helicopter?

It's _____ the bank.

3 _____ the car?

It's _____ the shopping centre.

4 _____ the train?

It's _____ the plane.

5 _____ the traffic light?

It's _____ the zebra crossing.

Think **Read and draw lines. Then answer the questions.**

1 Start at the underground station.
Turn right. Turn left at the traffic
light. It's on the left. Where are you?

 hotel

2 Start at the restaurant. Turn right.
Turn left. It's on the right, opposite
the hotel. Where are you?

 _____

3 Start at the park. Cross the first zebra
crossing. Turn left. Go straight ahead.
It's on the right, opposite the square.
Where are you?

 _____

4 Start at the shopping centre.
Turn right and go straight
ahead. Turn left at the zebra
crossing. Go straight ahead.
Turn right at the zebra crossing.
Stop. Where are you?

 _____

5 Start at the square. Turn right.
Turn left. Go straight ahead.
Turn left after the museum.
Stop. Where are you?

 _____

 Look at activity 5. Write the directions.

1 Where's the museum? Start at the bank. _Turn_ _____

 _____

2 Where's the bus station? Start at the square. _____

 _____

3 Where's the park? Start at the cinema. _____

 _____

Skills: *Writing*

7 Read the paragraph and write the words.

museum   restaurants   ~~square~~   shopping centre   station

My favourite city

My favourite city is Tokyo in Japan. You can see a statue of a famous dog, Hachiko, in a **1** ___*square*___ . I like eating at cafés and **2** _____ there too. I also like going shopping in Harajuku. You can see lots of beautiful clothes at the **3** _____ .

Yoyogi Park is next to the underground **4** _____ . You can see bands playing music. It's very exciting!

The art **5** _____ is opposite the park on the left. You can see old Japanese art there.

8 (About Me) **Answer the questions.**

1 What's your favourite city?

_____

2 What do you like doing there?

_____

3 Where do you like going?

_____

4 What can you see there?

_____

9 (About Me) **Write about your favourite city or town.**

My favourite city is _____

_____

_____

_____

10 (About Me) **Ask and answer with a friend.**

What's your favourite city?   My favourite city is Madrid.

11 Read and match.

1 Stop at the traffic lights.
2 Turn left at the museum and go straight ahead.
3 Can we have the net, please?
4 ~~I know. Follow me.~~

a

Look at this! A net!

Football competition Harton Park
How many goals can you score?

Where's Harton?

4

b

Be careful everyone.

to Harton

Yes, OK.

c

Excuse me. How do you get to the park?

Thanks.

MUSEUM

___

d

___

It's for the adventure playground.

OK!

12 Look at activity 11. Write *yes* or *no*.

1 The museum is near the park. _yes_

2 Tom knows where Harton is. _____

3 It is safe to stop at the traffic lights. _____

4 They turn right at the museum. _____

5 They get a net at the park. _____

13 Look and tick the pictures that show the value: cycle safely.

14 Colour the words that sound like *surf*. Then answer the question.

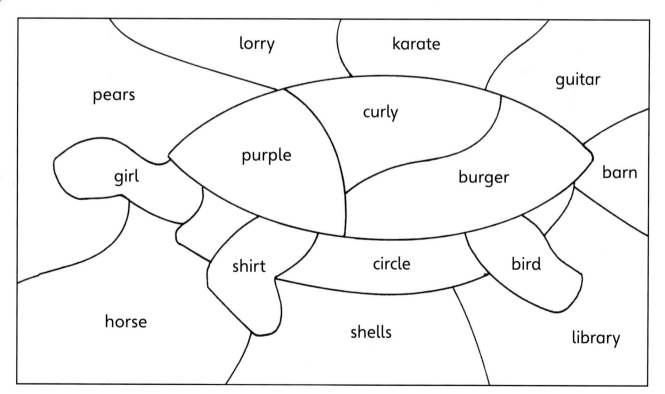

What is it? _____

What 3D shapes can you see?

1 Read and match.

1 There are four cylinders.   `b`

2 There's a big cube and a small pyramid.

3 There's a big sphere and four small spheres.

4 There are four small cones and a pyramid.

5 There are four small cones and a cube.

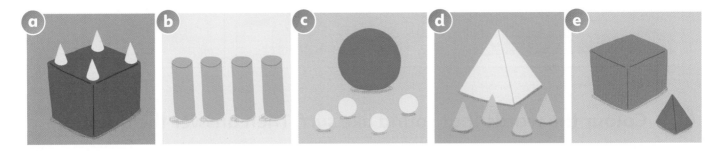

2 Draw the 3D shapes.

1 Draw a museum. It's a cube. It's got two cone shapes and five cylinders.
2 Draw an underground station. It's a cylinder. It's got eight spheres and three pyramids.
3 Draw a hotel. It's a pyramid. It's got a cube at the front and a sphere on top.

Evaluation

1 Look and complete the questions and answers.

1 Where's the bank?

It's ___next to___ the hotel.

2 Where's the art gallery?

It's _____ the museum.

3 Where's the shopping centre?

It's _____ the book shop.

4 Where's the restaurant?

It's _____ the bus station.

2 (About Me) **Complete the sentences about this unit.**

1 I can talk about _____ .

2 I can write about _____ .

3 My favourite part is _____ .

3 (Puzzle) **Guess what it is.**

You stop when it's red. You go when it's green. What is it?

_____

Go to page 93 and write the answer.

Review Units 1 and 2

1 Read and draw.

This is Ray. He's a boy. He's **1** metre 50 centimetres tall. He's got curly brown hair. He's got glasses. His favourite sport is football.

2 Look at activity 1. Write the questions and answers.

1 Is Ray a boy or a girl?

   He's a boy.

2 _____

   He's **1** metre 50 centimetres.

3 _____ ?

   He's tall. He's got curly hair.

4 _____ fair hair?

   No, _____ .

5 _____ glasses?

   Yes, _____ .

6 _____ football?

   Yes, _____ .

3 Look and write.

1 Me

I'm _not very good at ice skating_ .

2 Me

_____ good at _____ .

3 Henri

He's _____ .

4 Lori

She's _____ .

4 (About Me) **Look at activity 3 and write about you.**

1 I'm _____ at ice skating.   3 _____

2 I'm _____ at bowling.   4 _____

5 **Look and complete the questions and answers. Then match.**

3 _Are you good at singing?_

No, _____ .

☐ _____ good at playing the piano?

Yes, _____ .

☐ _____ good at playing the recorder?

Yes, _____ .

☐ _____ good at playing the guitar?

No, _____ .

6 (Think) **Do the word puzzle. Then use the letters in the circles to answer the question.**

Across →

Down ↓

1 b u s | s t a t i o n

Which letter of the alphabet has got

lots of w _ _ _ _ ? The ' _ _ _ _ ' (sea).

29

3 At work

1 (Think) **Write the words. Then tick the odd one out.**

1

 ✓

actor   doctor   nurse

2

3

4

~~actor~~
actor
artist
bus driver
businessman
businesswoman
~~doctor~~
~~nurse~~
pilot
singer
singer
vet

2 **Look at activity 1. Write the words.**

Where do they work?		
in a hospital	in an office	in a theatre
doctor		

My picture dictionary Go to page 87: Find and write the new words.

3 Put the words in order. Then match.

1 do / your / What / does / dad / ?

What does your dad do?

She's / businesswoman / a / .

_____

2 aunt / does / do / your / What / ?

_____

vet / a / He's / .

_____

3 do / your / does / uncle / What / ?

_____

a / She's / pilot / .

_____

4 does / mum / What / do / your / ?

_____

actor / He's / an / .

He's an actor.

4 Look at activity 3. Complete the questions and answers.

1 (your uncle) _____Where does_____ he _____work?_____

_____He works_____ in an animal hospital.

2 (your aunt) _____ she _____ ?

_____ in a plane.

3 (your dad) _____ he _____ ?

_____

4 (your mum) _____ she _____ ?

_____

5 Write the name of a famous person. Then ask and answer with a friend.

What does she do?   She's a singer.

Where does she work?   She works in theatres and studios.

6 **Read and number.**

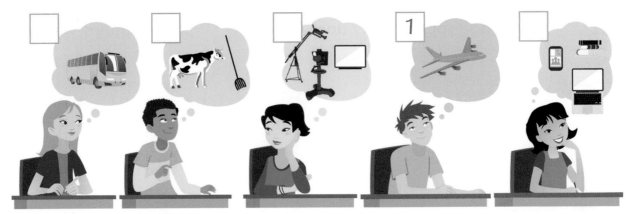

1 I want to be a pilot.
2 I want to be a bus driver.
3 I want to be a businesswoman.

4 I want to be an actor.
5 I want to be a farmer.

7 **Look and write the questions and answers.**

1 What do you ___*want to be?*___

   I ___*want to be*___ a doctor.

2 _____

   _____

3 What do you _____ ?

   I _____ a singer.

4 _____

   _____

8 (About Me) **Answer the questions.**

1 Do you want to be a vet?

   _____

2 Do you want to be a footballer?

   _____

3 Do you want to be a pilot?

   _____

4 What do you want to be?

   _____

Skills: *Writing*

9 **Read the paragraph and write the words.**

~~want to~~   Maths   like   office   don't   planes   want to

I ^{1} _want to_ be a pilot. I ^{2}_____ seeing new things and I like learning about new places. I'm good at ^{3}_____ . I ^{4}_____ want to work in an ^{5}_____ . I ^{6}_____ work on a plane and fly in the sky. I want to work with ^{7}_____ !

10 (About Me) **Answer the questions.**

1 What do you want to be?

_____

2 What do you like doing?

_____

3 What are you good at?

_____

4 Where do you want to work?

_____

5 Who/What do you want to work with?

_____

11 (About Me) **Write about what you want to be.**

I want to be _____

_____

_____

_____

_____

12 (About Me) **Ask and answer with a friend.**

What do you want to be?   I want to be a farmer.

13 Read and write the words.

Yes, please.   ~~farmer~~   don't need to   animals   Shall I   farm   help me

a Let's ask my uncle. He's a _farmer_ . He's got some on his farm.

b Hi, Uncle Jim. Can we have some rope and tyres, please?

What for?

For the adventure playground.

OK, but can you _____ with the _____ first?

c _____ feed the hens?

OK!

_____ . Lucas, can you give some water to the horse?

d Shall I take the dog for a walk?

We _____ , Anna. Let's look at the goats.

14 Look at activity 13. Circle the answers.

1 Lily's uncle is a _____ .
   a (farmer)   **b** rope   **c** tyre

2 The ropes and tyres are for _____ .
   a Lily's uncle   **b** the farm   **c** the adventure playground

3 Uncle Jim wants help with _____ .
   a the adventure playground   **b** the animals   **c** the farm

4 The water is for _____ .
   a the hens   **b** the horse   **c** the goats

5 They need to feed _____ .
   a the dog   **b** the horse   **c** the hens

15 Read and tick the activities that show the value: take care of pets and animals.

1 ✓ love
2 ☐ borrow
3 ☐ give water

4 ☐ play with
5 ☐ take for a walk
6 ☐ do homework

7 ☐ feed
8 ☐ watch TV
9 ☐ brush hair

16 Circle the words with the *cr* sound.

What type of work is it?

1 **Match the types of work with the pictures.**

a outdoor work   **b** factory work   **c** transport work   **d** shop work

 1   b

 2

 3

 4

 5

 6

2 **Look and put the pictures in the correct order.**

a outdoor work   **b** factory work   **c** transport work   **d** shop work

 1

_____ d _____

 2

Evaluation

1 Find and circle the words. Then match.

artistbusdriverbusinesswomannursebusinessmanactordoctorvetpilotsinger

2 (Think) Look and complete the questions and answers.

What does your grandfather _do_ ?

He's a ___nurse___ . _____ he work?

He works in a _____ .

_____ mum _____ ?

She's an _____ . _____ she work?

She works on ___TV___ .

3 (About Me) Complete the sentences about this unit.

1 I can talk about _____ .

2 I can write about _____ .

3 My favourite part is _____ .

4 (Puzzle) Guess what it is.

This person can fly a helicopter.

Who is it? _____

Go to page 93 and write the answer.

4 Wild animals

1 Look and tick the correct words.

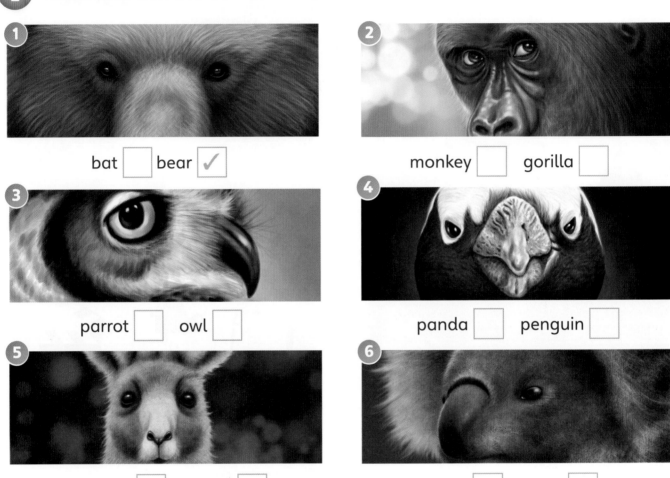

1. bat ☐ bear ✓

2. monkey ☐ gorilla ☐

3. parrot ☐ owl ☐

4. panda ☐ penguin ☐

5. kangaroo ☐ jaguar ☐

6. owl ☐ koala ☐

2 Write the words.

kangaroo bat penguin ~~parrot~~ panda jaguar

It can fly.	It's got a long tail.	It's black and white.
parrot		

My picture dictionary → Go to page 88: Find and write the new words.

3 **Read and choose the correct words.**

1 Bears — are smaller than / are bigger than → gorillas.

2 Kangaroos — are slower than / are quicker than — jaguars.

3 Koalas — are noisier than / are quieter than — bats.

4 Rabbits — are slower than / are quicker than — penguins.

5 Parrots — are noisier than / are quieter than — snails.

4 **Look and complete the sentences. Use the words in the box.**

1 Gorillas are _____*bigger*_____ than jaguars.

2 Gorillas are _____ than koalas.

3 Koalas _____ jaguars.

4 Jaguars _____ gorillas.

> big   small

5 Parrots are _____ than bats.

6 Bats are _____ than butterflies.

7 Butterflies _____ bats.

8 Bats _____ parrots.

> 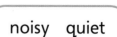 noisy   quiet

5 (Think) **Read and circle the correct words.**

1 Are koalas **quicker** / (**slower**) than gorillas?   Yes, they are.

2 Are owls **smaller** / **bigger** than pandas?   No, they aren't.

3 Are horses **taller** / **shorter** than gorillas?   No, they aren't.

4 Are parrots **noisier** / **quieter** than guinea pigs?   Yes, they are.

5 Are cats **longer** / **shorter** than jaguars?   No, they aren't.

6 **Look and use the words to complete the questions.**

quick / slow

1 Are jaguars ___quicker than___ tortoises?
Yes, they are.

2 Are tortoises _____ jaguars?
Yes, they are.

tall / short

3 Are kangaroos _____ penguins?
No, they aren't.

4 Are penguins _____ kangaroos?
No, they aren't.

long / short

5 Are dolphins _____ caterpillars?
Yes, they are.

6 Are caterpillars _____ dolphins?
Yes, they are.

7 (About Me) **Complete the questions and write the answers.**

~~tall~~   short   quiet   noisy

1 Are you _____*taller than*_____ your friend?   _____

2 Are you _____ your friend?   _____

3 _____ your friend?   _____

4 _____ your friend?   _____

Skills: *Writing*

8 **Read the paragraph and write the words.**

taller   spots   Africa   ~~long~~   leaves

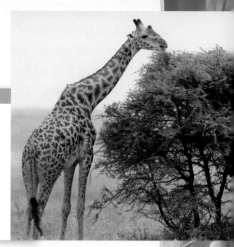

My favourite animal
My favourite animal is the giraffe. Giraffes are very tall. They are brown and white and they've got a ¹___*long*___ neck and ²_____ . They come from ³_____ . They are wild animals, not pets. They eat ⁴_____ . They are ⁵_____ than a tree.

9 **(About Me) Answer the questions.**

1   What's your favourite animal?

_____

2   What does it look like?

_____

3   Where does it come from?

_____

4   What does it eat?

_____

5   Is it taller than a tree?

_____

10 **(About Me) Write about your favourite animal.**

My favourite animal _____

_____

_____

_____

11 **(About Me) Guess your friend's favourite animal.**

It's smaller than a cat. It's slower than a guinea pig. It eats grass.

Is it a tortoise?

Yes, it is.

12 Read and number in order.

a
Grandpa, can you make an owl box for us?

Yes – you can help.

b
It's beautiful.

There you are! A house for an owl!

c
Where are the nails?

Here they are.

Can you pass them, please?

d
No, Anna. We need bigger boxes. Owls are bigger than other birds.

Are these owl boxes?

Let's make one.

e
Thank you. It's for the nature zone.

Wow! There are lots of boxes.

It's an owl town!

f
Are there bird boxes in your garden, Tom?

Yes, there are. But there aren't many.

1

13 Look at activity 12. Answer the questions.

1 What do they want to make? _____ An owl box.

2 Why do they need to make one? _____

3 Who helps them to make it? _____

4 What do they need to make it? _____

5 What's an owl box? _____

14 **Look and tick the pictures that show the value: look after nature.**

1

2

3

4

5

6

15 **Look and write the words with the *fr* sound.**

1 _____

2 _____

3 _____

a   b   c

d   e   f

What animal group is it?

1 Read the questions and write the words in the correct boxes.

snake frog panda ~~parrot~~ | fish amphibian ~~bird~~ mammal reptile

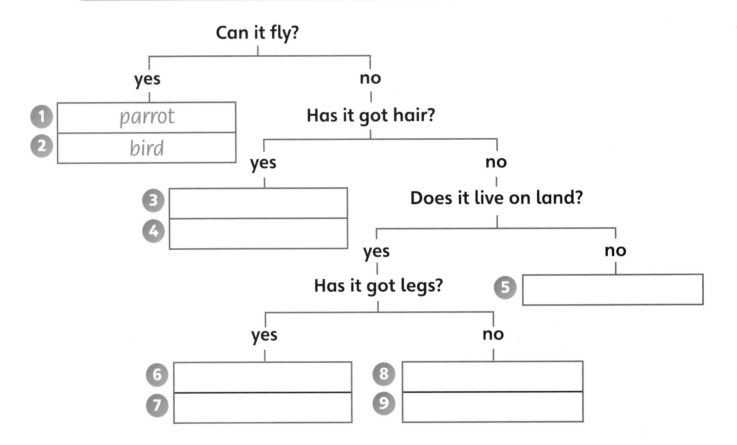

Can it fly?

yes

1 *parrot*
2 *bird*

no

Has it got hair?

yes

3
4

no

Does it live on land?

yes

Has it got legs?

no

5

yes

6
7

no

8
9

2 Look at activity 1. Write about a reptile, a bird, a mammal and an amphibian.

1 *A snake is a reptile. It can't fly and it hasn't got hair. It lives on land.*

2 _____

3 _____

4 _____

Evaluation

 1 **Think** **Find and circle ten animal words→↓. Use the extra letters to answer the question.**

Where do gorillas come from?
A _ _ _ _ _ _

j	a	g	u	a	r	c	b	p	i
p	a	r	r	o	t	f	e	a	k
g	o	r	i	l	l	a	a	n	o
o	w	l	b	a	t	a	r	d	a
p	e	n	g	u	i	n	r	a	l
a	k	a	n	g	a	r	o	o	a

2 **Look and complete the sentences.**

big small quiet quick

1 Gorillas are ___bigger___ than koalas.

2 Owls are _____ than parrots.

3 Bats _____ kangaroos.

4 Jaguars _____ penguins.

3 **About Me** **Complete the sentences about this unit.**

1 I can talk about _____ .

2 I can write about _____ .

3 My favourite part is _____ .

4 **Puzzle** **Guess what it is.**

It's big and black and white. It eats leaves. What is it? _____

Go to page 93 and write the answer.

Review Units 3 and 4

1 Look and tick the correct answers.

1 What do you want to be?

☑ **a** I want to be a teacher.

☐ **b** I want to be a businessman.

2 Do you want to be a singer?

☐ **a** Yes, I do.

☐ **b** No, I don't. I want to be a farmer.

3 Do you want to be a footballer?

☐ **a** Yes, I do.

☐ **b** No, I don't. I want to be a bus driver.

4 What do you want to be?

☐ **a** I want to be an actor.

☐ **b** I want to be a businesswoman.

2 Read and complete the conversation.

Gemma: _What does your_ mum _____ ?

Paul: She's an _____ . She likes drawing and painting.

Gemma: _____ she _____ ?

Paul: She works in a studio.

Gemma: Do you _____ an artist too?

Paul: No, I don't. I like Maths. I _____ a teacher.

Paul   Gemma

3 **Look and write the questions and answers.**

short long small ~~big~~

wallaby

kangaroo

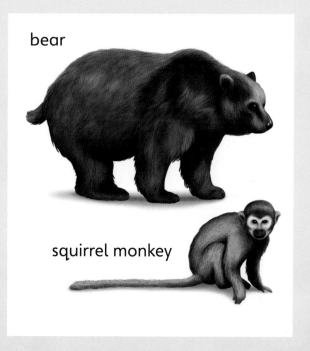

bear

squirrel monkey

1 Are kangaroos _____bigger than_____ wallabies? Yes, they are.

2 Are wallabies _____ kangaroos? Yes, _____ .

3 Are squirrel monkey tails _____ bear tails? No, _____ .

4 Are bear tails _____ squirrel monkey tails? No, _____ .

4 **Use the words to complete the questions. Then write answers.**

~~small~~ noisy quick big fast

1 Are you _smaller than_ a gorilla?   _Yes, I am._

2 Are you _____ a parrot?   _____

3 Are you _____ a jaguar?   _____

4 Are you _____ a koala?   _____

5 Are you _____ a tortoise?   _____

5 Food and drink

1 Look and write the words.

 1 pous
soup

 2 ladsa

 3 zipza

 4 satap

 5 turgoyh

 6 sispcr

 7 tuicisb

 8 tuns

 9 eat

 10 eofefc

2 (Think) **What do they want for lunch? Read and then write the words.**

Tim: I want pizza for lunch!

Gina: I don't. I want pasta and salad.

Tim: I want salad, too. And yoghurt. I like yoghurt.

Gina: I want tea and a biscuit, too.

Tim: I want tea, too.

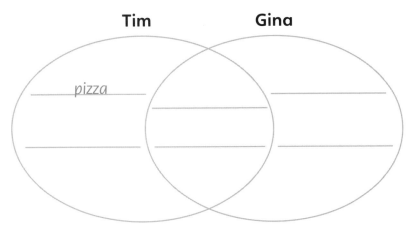

Tim   Gina

pizza

My picture dictionary ➡ Go to page 89: Find and write the new words.

3 Look and count. Then complete the sentences.

0	1–2	3–4	5–6
never	sometimes	usually	always

breakfast   lunch   dinner

1 I _____usually_____ have tea for lunch.

2 I _____ have milk for lunch

3 I _____ have fish for dinner.

4 I _____ have coffee for breakfast.

5 I _____ have apples for breakfast.

4 Look at activity 3. Then complete the sentences.

1 She _____always has toast_____ for breakfast.

2 She _____ for lunch.

3 She _____ for dinner.

4 She _____ for dinner.

5 She _____ for breakfast.

5 (About Me) Complete the sentences.

1 I _____ for breakfast.

2 I _____ for lunch.

3 I _____ for dinner.

6 Look and complete the questions and answers.

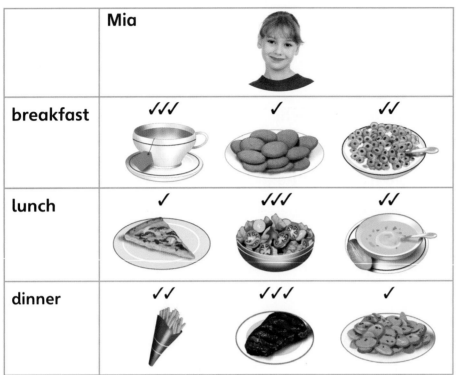

	Mia		
breakfast	✓✓✓	✓	✓✓
lunch	✓	✓✓✓	✓✓
dinner	✓✓	✓✓✓	✓

	never
✓	sometimes
✓✓	usually
✓✓✓	every day

1   _____How often do you have_____ cereal for breakfast?

I _____usually_____ have cereal for breakfast.

2   _____ salad for lunch?

I have salad for lunch _____ .

3   _____ meat for dinner?

I _____ meat for dinner _____ .

4   _____ carrots for dinner?

_____

5   _____ yoghurt for breakfast?

_____

7 (About Me) Answer the questions.

1   How often do you have cereal for breakfast?   _____

2   How often do you have salad for lunch?   _____

3   How often do you have fish for dinner?   _____

Skills: *Writing*

8 **Make a lunch diary. Write what you eat and drink for lunch every day.**

biscuits coffee crisps nuts pasta pizza salad soup tea yoghurt

Monday	Tuesday	Wednesday	Thursday	Friday

9 **Look at activity 8. Answer the questions.**

1 What do you usually have for lunch? _____

2 What do you sometimes have for lunch? _____

3 What do you eat or drink every day for lunch? _____

4 What do you never have for lunch? _____

5 Do you have a healthy lunch? _____

10 **Write about what you eat for lunch.**

I usually eat _____

_____

_____

_____

_____

11 **Ask and answer with a friend.**

What do you eat for lunch?

I usually have rice and beans. Sometimes I drink milk.

12 Read and match.

1 Can I have two, please?
2 ~~£15! That's a lot of money.~~
3 Let's wash our hands first.
4 How about selling fruit?

How can we get £15?

2

Week 5
We need bean bags.

£15

I can give you £10 to buy the fruit.

Thanks, Dad!

Good idea. Come on, Anna.

OK.

How much is the fruit salad?

It's one pound.

Yes, of course. Here you are.

£1

13 Look at activity 12. Write *yes* or *no*.

1 They need to get a lot of money. _____yes_____

2 Lucas's dad gives them money to buy fruit. _____

3 Washing your hands before touching food is a good idea. _____

4 The fruit salad costs two pounds. _____

5 Lucas's grandma sells fruit salad. _____

14 Look and tick the pictures that show the value: be clean around food.

15 Circle the words with the *ar* sound.

Where does water come from?

1 **Look and write.**

~~cloud~~ glacier mountain rain river sea spring well

1 _cloud_

2 _____

3 _____

4 _____

5 _____

6 _____

7 _____

8 _____

2 **Complete the sentences about water.**

1 Water comes from c_louds_ and r_____ .

2 Some people drink water from a w_____ or a s_____ .

3 We can see a g_____ in the mountains.

4 A r_____ goes to the s_____ .

Evaluation

1 Look and match.

1	yoghurt	h	6	crisps
2	pasta		7	salad
3	tea		8	coffee
4	nuts		9	pizza
5	soup		10	biscuit

a   b   c   d   e   f   g   h   i   j

2 Look and write.

	Monday	Tuesday	Wednesday	Thursday	Friday
	cake	cake	crisps	cake	cake
Emile	nuts	nuts	cake	nuts	coffee

1 How often does Emile have crisps?　　　　　　Sometimes.

2 How often does he have cake?　　　　　　_____

3 How often does he have pizza?　　　　　　_____

4 How often does he have nuts?　　　　　　_____

5 How often does he have coffee?　　　　　　_____

3 Complete the sentences about this unit.

1 I can talk about _____ .

2 I can write about _____ .

3 My favourite part is _____ .

4 Guess what it is.

It's a drink. It's dark brown. It's usually hot. It's not tea. What is it?

_____

Go to page 93 and write the answer.

1 Look and write the words.

backache
cold
cough
earache
headache
~~sore throat~~
stomachache
temperature
toothache

sore throat

_____   _____   _____   _____   _____

2 Look and complete the sentences.

1 Dan's got a
   stomachache .

2 Grace's got a
   _____ .

3 Ann's got a
   _____ .

4 May's got a
   _____ .

5 Tony's got a
   _____ .

Ann   Tony   Grace   May   Dan

My picture dictionary Go to page 90: Find and write the new words.

3 Look and write.

What's the ___matter___ , Kelly?

I've got a ___cold___ , an ___earache___ and a

_____ .

What's the _____ , Bill?

I've got a _____ , a _____ _____ and a

_____ .

What's the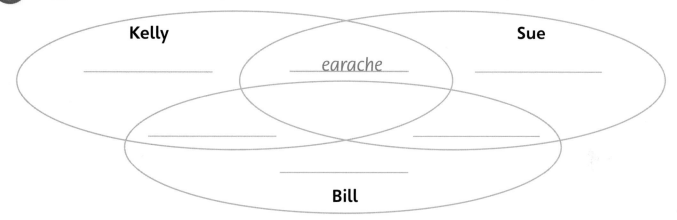

_____ , Sue?

I've got an _____ , a _____ and a

_____ .

4 (Think) Look at activity 3. Write the words.

Kelly   Sue

_____   ___earache___   _____

_____   _____

_____

Bill

5 Look and write the questions and answers.

1 What's the ___matter___ ?

I've got ___an earache___ .

2 What's the _____ ?

I've got _____ .

3 What's the _____ ?

I've got _____ .

4 _____ ?

_____

Grammar **57**

6 Complete the questions and say why you can't.

1 _Can you_ go kayaking today?

No, I _can't_ . I've got a _temperature_ .

2 _____ go snowboarding today?

No, I _____ . I've got a _____ .

3 _____ go to the museum today?

_____

4 _____ play football today?

_____

5 _____ go swimming today?

_____

7 Complete the sentences. Use the words in the box.

a cold   an earache   a backache   a temperature

1 Can you go bowling today?

No, _I can't_ .

I've got a backache .

2 Can you go kayaking today?

No, _____ .

_____

3 Can you go to the cinema tonight?

No, _____ .

_____

4 Can you go swimming tomorrow?

No, _____ .

_____

Skills: *Writing*

8 **Read the paragraph and write the words.**

favourite wash yoghurt lunch need

Apple and nut salad is my ¹___favourite___ salad. It's healthy because apples and nuts are good for you. I sometimes have this salad for ²_____ .

- You ³_____ apples, nuts, cheese, yoghurt and carrots.
- ⁴_____ the fruit and vegetables. Cut the apples, carrots and cheese.
- Add some ⁵_____ .

9 (About Me) **Answer the questions.**

1 What's your favourite healthy food or drink?

_____

2 Why is it healthy?

_____

3 What do you need?

_____

4 How do you make it?

_____

5 How often do you eat/drink it?

_____

10 (About Me) **Write a recipe for your favourite healthy food or drink.**

_____

_____

_____

_____

11 (About Me) **Ask and answer with a friend.**

What's your favourite healthy food or drink?

My favourite healthy food is salad.

Read and write the words.

> headache   ~~competition~~   leg hurts   very good   OK now

a ...reboarding competition today Win a skateboard!

It's a <u>competition</u> !

Go, Chris!

b Oh dear!

Are you OK, Chris?

Yes, I think so. My _____ , but I'm OK. Don't worry.

c Have you got a _____ , Chris?

No, I'm _____ .

But where's your skateboard?

d Well done, Max!

Sorry, Chris!

That's OK! I'm good at skateboarding, but Max is _____ !

13 **Look at activity 12. Circle the correct words.**

1 Chris has a skateboarding **club** / (competition) / **team**.
2 Chris's **leg** / **head** / **ear** hurts.
3 Chris says he hasn't got a **backache** / **stomachache** / **headache**.
4 Max is **really bad** / **OK** / **really good** at skateboarding.
5 **Chris** / **Tom** / **Lily** is a good sport.

14 Look and tick the pictures that show the value: be a good sport.

1 Good game. ✓

2 I'm number 1! ☐

3 You're not very good. Wah! ☐

4 Well done! ☐

15 Connect the words with the *sp* sound.

What can we use plants for?

1 Read and match.

1 We can use trees for fuel. `c`

2 We can use plants to give us cereal. ☐

3 We can use the fruit from plants for medicine. ☐

4 We can use the wood from trees to give us shelter. ☐

5 We can use plants to make fabric. ☐

2 Draw a plant. Then write three ways we can use your plant.

1 _____

_____

2 _____

_____

3 _____

_____

Evaluation

1 (Think) **Look and then complete the sentences.**

Ed
stomachache

Kate
sore
throat

cold

Will
temperature

1   _____What's the matter_____ with Will?

He's got a _____cold_____ and

a _____ .

2   _____ Ed?

He's got a _____ and

a _____ .

3   _____ Kate?

_____ and

a _____ .

2 **Read and then complete the answers.**

1   Can you go to the cinema today?

(My head hurts.)
No, I __can't__ . I've got a _headache_ .

2   Can you go to the café tonight?

(My tooth hurts.)
No, I _____ . I've got a _____ .

3   Can you play basketball this afternoon?

(My back hurts.)
_____

3 (About Me) **Complete the sentences about this unit.**

1   I can talk about _____ .

2   I can write about _____ .

3   My favourite part is _____ .

4 (Puzzle) **Guess what it is.**

Eating a lot of food can give you

a _____ . What is it?

Go to page 93 and write the answer.

Review Units 5 and 6

1 Complete the sentences.

breakfast / me

lunch / Kim

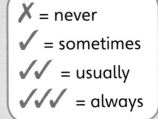

X = never
✓ = sometimes
✓✓ = usually
✓✓✓ = always

1 She ___sometimes has___ soup for lunch.

2 I _____ yoghurt for breakfast.

3 She _____ rice for lunch.

4 I _____ tea for breakfast.

5 She _____ a sandwich for lunch.

6 I _____ toast for breakfast.

2 Think Read and then write the words.

Leo and Carol usually have pizza for lunch and Billy usually has fish. Sometimes Leo has a sandwich and sometimes Billy and Carol have salad. Leo and Billy usually have crisps and Carol usually has yoghurt. Carol, Billy and Leo always drink tea for lunch.

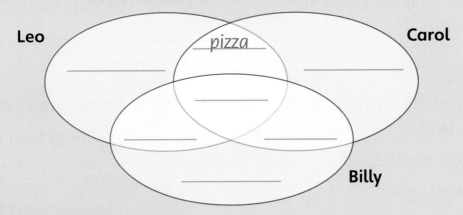

Leo

Carol

pizza

Billy

3 About Me Answer the questions.

1 What do you always have for breakfast? _____

2 What do you usually have for lunch? _____

3 What do you sometimes have for dinner? _____

4 What do you never have for dinner? _____

4 (Think) **Find the letters and write the words. Then match.**

a	b	c	d	e	f	g	h	i	j	k	l	m
■	▼	◆	✕	●	✚	★	◗	▮	⁞	↓	♥	✳

n	o	p	q	r	s	t	u	v	w	x	y	z
()	▲	⬟	◖	▲	/	▬	↑	❀	Ɛ	◆▶	)	⚡

1 ◆ ▲ ↑ ★ ◗
_c o u g h_

2 ◗ ● ▮ ✕ ■ ◆ ◗ ●
_____

3 ▬ ● ✳ ⬟ ● ▲ ■ ▬ ↑ ▲ ●
_____

4 ▬ ▲ ▲ ▬ ◗ ■ ◆ ◗ ●
_____

5 ◆ ▲ ♥ ✕
_____

6 / ▲ ▲ ●   ▬ ◗ ▲ ▲ ■ ▬
_____

7 ▼ ▮ ◆ ↓ ▮ ◆ ◗ ●
_____

8 / ▬ ▲ ✳ ■ ◆ ◗ ■ ◆ ◗ ●
_____

9 ● ▮ ▲ ■ ◆ ◗ ●
_____

a

f [1]

b

g

c

h

d

i

e

5 **Read and complete the answers.**

> Oh dear   ~~I think so~~   I don't think so   Oh, good   Don't worry

1 Are you OK?
Yes, ____I think so____ .
_____ .
_____ !

2 Are you OK?
No, _____ . I've got an earache.
_____ !

7 Buildings

1 Look and number.

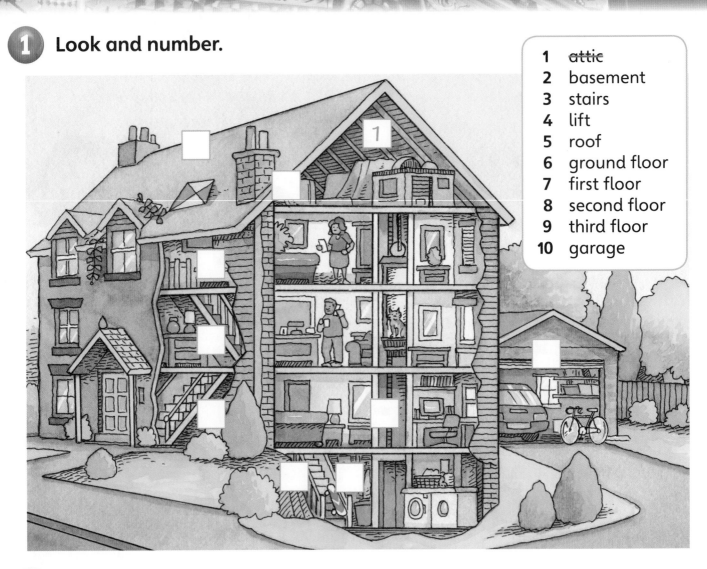

1	~~attic~~
2	basement
3	stairs
4	lift
5	roof
6	ground floor
7	first floor
8	second floor
9	third floor
10	garage

2 Look at activity 1. Write the words.

1 There's a kite on the _____roof_____ .

2 There's a cat in the _____ .

3 There's a car in the _____ .

4 There's a skateboard on the _____ .

5 There's a man on the _____ _____ .

6 There's a woman on the _____ _____ .

My picture dictionary Go to page 91: Find and write the new words.

3 **Put the words in order. Then write the number.**

1 you / Where / morning / yesterday / were / ?

Where were you yesterday morning?

the / was / I / kitchen / in / .

I was in the kitchen.

2 were / afternoon / you / Where / yesterday / ?

_____

second / on / I / the / was / floor / .

_____

3 yesterday / you / evening / were / Where / ?

_____

in / I / room / the / was / living / .

_____

4 morning / were / yesterday / Where / you / ?

_____

was / I / in / garage / the / .

_____

5 night / were / you / last / Where / ?

_____

bedroom / floor / I / in / my / on / the / third / was / .

_____

4 **Answer the questions.**

1 Where were you yesterday morning?

_____

2 Where were you yesterday afternoon?

_____

3 Where were you yesterday evening?

_____

4 Where were you last night?

_____

5 **Look and tick *Yes, I was* or *No, I wasn't*.**

	Yes, I was.	No, I wasn't.
1 Were you at the sports field yesterday morning?	☐	☑
2 Were you at the beach yesterday morning?	☐	☐
3 Were you at a restaurant yesterday afternoon?	☐	☐
4 Were you at home last night?	☐	☐
5 Were you at the cinema yesterday evening?	☐	☐

10 o'clock   *at the beach*

3 o'clock   *at the shopping centre*

6 o'clock   *at the sports field*

11 o'clock   *at home*

6 **Look and write.**

yesterday morning	yesterday afternoon	yesterday evening	last night

1 ___Were you___ at the sports centre yesterday evening?   Yes, ___I was___ .

2 _____ at home yesterday afternoon?   No, _____ .

3 _____ at school yesterday afternoon?   Yes, _____ .

4 _____ in your bedroom yesterday morning?   Yes, _____ .

5 _____ at the cinema last night?   No, _____ .

7 **Answer the questions.**

1 Were you at school yesterday morning? _____

2 Were you at the library yesterday afternoon? _____

3 Were you on the bus yesterday evening? _____

4 Were you at a restaurant last night? _____

Skills: *Writing*

8 **Read the text. Circle the answers to the questions.**

On Saturday morning, I was (at the park) with my dog. Then I was at a café

at lunchtime. In the afternoon, I was at the sports centre. It was exciting.

I love playing basketball! In the evening, I was at the cinema.

1   Where were you in the morning?
2   Where were you at lunchtime?
3   Where were you in the afternoon?
4   Where were you in the evening?

9 (About Me) **Look at activity 8. Choose a day. Answer the questions for you.**

Day: _____

1   _____
2   _____
3   _____
4   _____

10 (About Me) **Write about your day.**

_____
_____
_____
_____
_____
_____
_____
_____

11 (About Me) **Ask and answer with a friend.**

Where were you in the morning?   I was at school.

12 Read and number in order.

a No! It's a tortoise!
It looks like my cousin Kim's tortoise!
Let's call and ask her.

b Oh, Speedy! Thank you so much!
What can we give you for a reward?

c Hello. I think we've got your tortoise.
Great! Where was he?
He was in my garage!

d Here's my old bike. Oh dear!
Look. Is that a helmet?

1

e Have you got an old bike?
Yes, I have!
A helmet too, please!

f Hello?
Hello. It's Lily. Is Kim there, please?
Yes, she is. Just a minute.

13 Look at activity 12. Answer the questions.

1 Who has an old bike? _____Lily_____

2 Is it a helmet or a tortoise? _____

3 Whose tortoise is it? _____

4 Where was the tortoise? _____

5 What's the tortoise's name? _____

14 Look and tick the pictures that show the value: look after your possessions.

15 Colour the words with the letters *ck*.

What materials were buildings made of?

1 **Look and match.**

1

2

3

4

clay

stone

animal skins

wood

a

b

c

d

2 **Draw your house. Then write about the old building and your house.**

1 The old building was made of ___*stone*___ .
   My house is made of _____ .

2 The old building is _____ than
   my house.

3 The old building has got _____
   floors. My house has got _____
   floors.

4 I don't think the old building has
   got a _____ .

5 My house has got a _____ .

Old stone castle.

My house.

Evaluation

1 **Do the word puzzle.**

Across →

1 You can put a car and a bicycle here.
3 It's below the third floor.
5 It's between the second floor and the attic.
7 It's below the ground floor.
8 It's above the ground floor.

Down ↓

2 It's where you usually come in the house.
4 It's above the third floor and below the roof.
6 It's above the attic.

¹ g a r a g e

2 **Complete the questions and answers.**

1 **Mark:** Where ___*were you*___ yesterday morning?

2 **Eva:** _____ at the beach.

3 **Mark:** Where were you in the afternoon?

4 **Eva:** _____ at the cinema.

5 **Mark:** _____ at a restaurant in the evening?

6 **Eva:** No, _____ . I was at home.

I was
I wasn't
~~were you~~
Were you
I was

3 **Complete the sentences about this unit.**

1 I can talk about _____ .

2 I can write about _____ .

3 My favourite part is _____ .

4 **Guess what it is.**

It's quicker than the stairs.

What is it? _____

Go to page 93 and write the answer.

1 **Look and match.**

1 snowy [*a*]   **2** cloudy [ ]   **3** windy [ ]   **4** sunny [ ]

5 foggy [ ]   **6** cold [ ]   **7** hot [ ]   **8** rainy [ ]

2 **Write the words.**

~~cold~~ hot warm

1 _cold_ **2** _____ **3** _____

My picture dictionary Go to page 92: Find and write the new words.

3 **Look and write.**

1 **Yesterday at 10:00.**

What was the weather like _yesterday morning_ ?

It was warm and rainy.

2 **Yesterday at 15:00.**

_____ the weather like _____ ?

_____ and _____ .

3 **Yesterday at 19:00.**

_____ the weather like _____ ?

_____

4 **Yesterday at 23:00.**

_____ the weather like _____ ?

_____ and _____ .

5 **Today.**

_____ ?

_____

4 (About Me) **Answer the questions.**

1 What was the weather like yesterday morning?

_____

2 What was the weather like last night?

_____

3 What's the weather like today?

_____

4 What's your favourite weather?

_____

5 (Think) **Read and match. Then write the days.**

1 Was it cold and foggy on Tuesday?
No, it wasn't. It was warm and windy.

2 Was it hot and rainy on Thursday?
No, it wasn't. It was cold and snowy.

Tuesday

3 Was it hot and sunny on Friday?
Yes, it was.

4 Was it cold and cloudy on Wednesday?
No, it wasn't. It was hot and rainy.

5 Was it hot and cloudy on Monday?
No, it wasn't. It was cold and cloudy.

6 **Look and complete the questions and answers.**

Tuesday   Thursday   Saturday   Sunday

1 _____ _Was it_ _____ warm and rainy on Tuesday?

Yes, it was. _____

2 _____ cold and snowy on Thursday?

_____

3 _____ hot and windy on Saturday?

No, it wasn't. It was _____ and _____ .

4 _____ cold and cloudy on Sunday?

_____

Skills: *Writing*

7 **Read about Jane's favourite festival and answer the questions.**

On Sunday I was at the Bristol hot-air balloon festival with my family. The balloon festival is every August. The weather's usually hot and sunny. The festival's really big and there are lots of beautiful hot-air balloons. You can fly in a hot-air balloon. I like taking photos of the balloons. They're fantastic!

1 What's Jane's favourite festival?

_____

2 When is it?

_____

3 What's the weather like?

_____

4 What can you see there?

_____

5 What can you do at the festival?

_____

8 **Answer the questions for you.**

1 _____

2 _____

3 _____

4 _____

5 _____

9 **Write about your favourite festival.**

_____

_____

_____

10 **Ask and answer with a friend.**

What's your favourite festival?

The Songkran water festival.

11 Read and match.

1 thank you for your hard work!
2 What time does the party start?
3 ~~Please come to the opening party on Saturday at four o'clock.~~
4 The adventure playground is now open!

12 Look at activity 11. Write *yes* or *no*.

1 The adventure playground is ready.   _yes_

2 The party's on Sunday.   _____

3 The party starts at five o'clock.   _____

4 Tom says thank you.   _____

5 Anna wants to be on TV.   _____

13 Look and tick the pictures that show the value: work hard and try your best.

1

2

 ✓

3

4

5

6

14 Look and write the words with the *nd* sound.

1 _____ *underground station* _____

2 _____

3 _____

4 _____

5 _____

What's the weather like around the world?

1 (Think) **Put the letters in order. Then match and write.**

1 There's a **rizlbazd** with lots of snow. | e | _blizzard_
2 It's very cloudy and there's a **rsairtnmo**. | □ | _____
3 There's a **uihrrance** above the sea. | □ | _____
4 There's a **rnootda**. It looks like a cone. | □ | _____
5 There's **hteundr** and **ghnlintig**. | □ | _____ and _____

a   b   c   d   e

2 **What's the weather like in Adventure Land? Draw and write.**

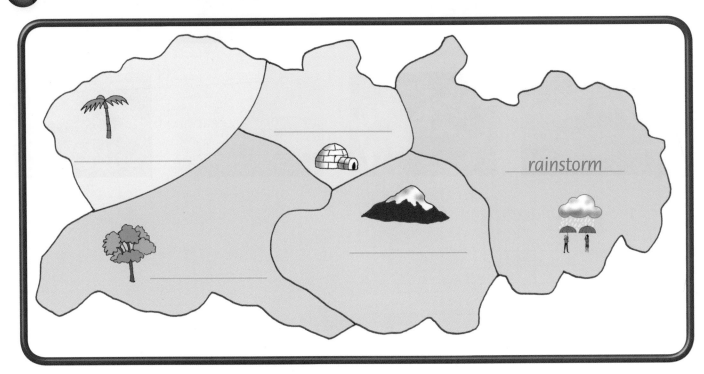

rainstorm

Evaluation

1 **Look and write.**

yesterday morning	yesterday afternoon	yesterday evening	last night

it was

it was

It was

it wasn't

Was it

Was it

~~What was~~

yesterday evening

~~yesterday morning~~

yesterday afternoon

Was it

1 _What was_ the weather like _yesterday morning_ ?

_____ cold and foggy.

2 _____ warm and windy last night?

No, _____ . It was cold and snowy.

3 _____ warm and windy _____ ? Yes, _____ .

4 _____ cold and rainy _____ ? Yes, _____ .

2 (About Me) **Complete the sentences about this unit.**

1 I can talk about _____ .

2 I can write about _____ .

3 My favourite part is _____ .

3 **Guess what it is.**

You need an umbrella for this weather. What is it?

_____

Go to page 93 and write the answer.

Review   Units 7 and 8

1 (Think) **Look and write.**

1 Where ___were you___ yesterday?

___I was___ at home.

2 Where _____ yesterday morning?

_____ in the _____ .

3 Where _____ yesterday afternoon?

_____ in the _____ .

4 Where _____ yesterday evening?

_____ in the _____ .

5 _____ last night?

_____ in my _____ .

2 **Look and write.**

1 ___Were you___ at the shopping centre in the afternoon?

___Yes, I was.___

2 _____ at the cinema yesterday afternoon?

_____

3 _____ at home yesterday morning?

_____

3 (About Me) **Answer the questions.**

1 Where were you yesterday morning? _____

2 Where were you yesterday afternoon? _____

3 Where were you yesterday evening? _____

4 Where were you last night? _____

Look and write.

yesterday today

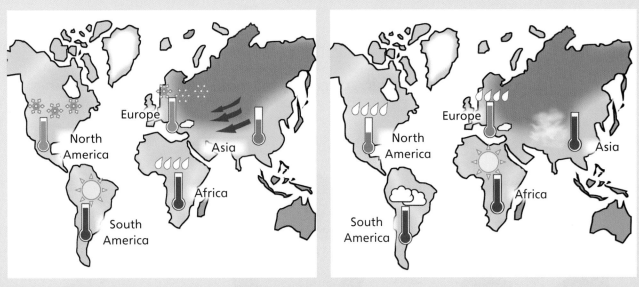

1 _____*What's*_____ the weather like in Africa today?

It's hot and sunny.

2 _____*What was*_____ the weather like in Africa yesterday?

It was hot and rainy.

3 _____ the weather like in North America today?

_____

4 _____ the weather like in North America yesterday?

_____

5 _____ the weather like in Asia today?

_____

6 _____ the weather like in Asia yesterday?

_____

7 _____ the weather like in South America today?

_____

8 _____ the weather like in South America yesterday?

_____

Welcome back!

dark hair   straight hair   glasses   fair hair   ~~curly hair~~   red hair

curly hair

_____

_____

_____

_____

_____

1 Fun sports

ice skating   sailing   skiing   kayaking   skateboarding   fishing
~~bowling~~   mountain biking   snowboarding

bowling

traffic light   museum   hotel   underground station   shopping centre
bus station   zebra crossing   square   ~~bank~~   restaurant

bank

_____

_____

_____

_____

_____

_____

_____

_____

_____

3 At work

vet ~~actor~~ singer doctor pilot businesswoman
artist bus driver nurse businessman

actor

parrot   gorilla   owl   koala   panda   jaguar   ~~bat~~   penguin   kangaroo   bear

bat

biscuit pizza pasta crisps nuts coffee soup tea salad yoghurt

biscuit

6 Health matters

temperature ~~backache~~ cold headache cough
stomachache sore throat earache toothache

backache

stairs basement third floor roof ~~attic~~ second floor
lift garage ground floor first floor

attic

foggy snowy hot rainy warm windy ~~cold~~ cloudy sunny

cold

Puzzle

1 Do the word puzzle.

Across →

3 (**Unit 4**) It's big and black and white. It eats leaves. What is it?
4 (**Welcome back!**) Hair that's not straight. What is it?
5 (**Unit 6**) Eating a lot of food can give you a … What is it?
7 (**Unit 1**) You need water and wind to do this sport. What is it?
8 (**Unit 7**) It's quicker than the stairs. What is it?

Down ↓

1 (**Unit 8**) You need an umbrella for this weather. What is it?
2 (**Unit 2**) You stop when it's red. You go when it's green. What is it? (two words)
3 (**Unit 3**) This person can fly a helicopter. Who is it?
6 (**Unit 5**) It's a drink. It's dark brown. It's usually hot. It's not tea. What is it?

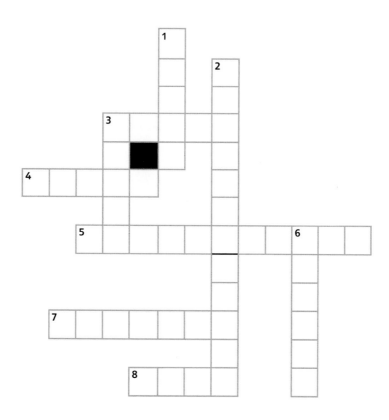

Story fun

1 **Match the objects to the words. Then match the words to the story units they come from.**

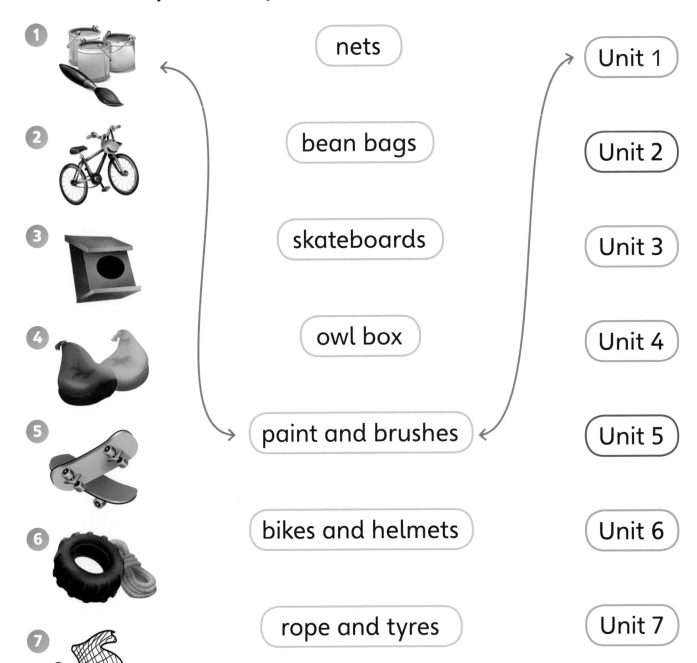

nets   Unit 1

bean bags   Unit 2

skateboards   Unit 3

owl box   Unit 4

paint and brushes   Unit 5

bikes and helmets   Unit 6

rope and tyres   Unit 7

2 Look and find the missing people and objects. Write the numbers in the boxes.

Thanks and Acknowledgements

The authors and publishers would like to thank the following contributors:

Blooberry Design: concept design, book design, page make-up

Christine Barton: editing

The authors and publishers acknowledge the following sources of copyright material and are grateful for the permissions granted. While every effort has been made, it has not always been possible to identify the sources of all the material used, or to trace all copyright holders. If any omissions are brought to our notice, we will be happy to include the appropriate acknowledgements on reprinting.

The authors and publishers would like to thank the following illustrators:

Pablo Gallego (Beehive Illustration): pp. 8, 16, 24, 34, 42, 52, 60, 70, 78, 94, 95; A Corazon Abierto (Sylvie Poggio): pp. 5, 13, 19, 25, 32, 46, 57, 58, 68, 75; Ilias Arahovitis (Beehive Illustration): pp. 13, 38, 40, 47, 54; Humberto Blanco (Sylvie Poggio): pp. 6, 12, 14, 20, 29, 32, 56, 65, 76, 82; Gareth Conway: pp. 10, 18, 26, 27, 36, 37, 45, 55; Marcus Cutler (Sylvie Poggio): pp. 17, 43, 53, 61, 71, 79; Graham Kennedy: pp. 49, 80, 83; Brian Lee: pp. 12, 20, 21, 22, 66, 67, 82; Monkey Feet: pp. 3, 84, 85, 86, 87, 88, 89, 90, 91, 92; Luke Newell: pp. 4, 7, 11, 28, 81.

The authors and publishers would like to thank the following for permission to reproduce photographs:

p. 4: Yi Lu/Viewstock/Corbis; p. 9 (1a): Chris Hill/Shutterstock; p. 9 (1b): Jaroslav Moravcik/Shutterstock; p. 9 (1c): mariait/Shutterstock; p. 9 (2a): Yuri Samsonov/Shutterstock; p. (2b): ThavornC/Shutterstock; p. 9 (2c): CreativeNature R.Zwerver/Shutterstock; p. 9 (3a): Paul Wishart/Shutterstock; p. 9 (3b): KK Art and Photography/Shutterstock; p. 9 (3c): Tymonko Galyna/Shutterstock; p. 9 (4a): smereka/Shutterstock; p. 9 (4b): lazlo/Shutterstock; p. 9 (4c): stacy2010ua/Shutterstock; p. 10: Thierry GRUN/Alamy; p. 11: exopixel/Shutterstock; p. 12: mediacolor's/Alamy; p. 14 (L): Andy Dean Photography/Shutterstock; p. 14 (R): keith morris/Shutterstock; p. 15: Lora liu/Shutterstock; p. 17 (1a): HomeStudio/Shutterstock; p. 17 (1b): stable/Shutterstock; p. 17 (1c): Fotoluminate LLC/Shutterstock; p. 17 (2a): Blend Images/Shutterstock; p. 17 (2b): Matt Jeppson/Shutterstock; p. 17 (2c): schantalao/Shutterstock; p. 17 (3a): Tracy Whiteside/Shutterstock; p. 17 (3b): exopixel/Shutterstock; p. 17 (3c): katatonia82/Shutterstock; p. 18: Mira/Alamy; p. 19: aragami12345s/Shutterstock; p. 23 (b/g): QQ7/Shutterstock; p. 23 (TR): Tetra Images/Alamy; p. 23 (TM): leungchopan/Shutterstock; p. 26: Zoonar GmbH/Alamy; p. 27: Claudio Divizia/Shutterstock; p. 29 (1): BestPix/Alamy; p. 29 (2): GOLFX/Shutterstock; p. 29 (3): Christina Kennedy/Alamy; p. 29 (4): ariadna de raadt/Shutterstock; p. 29 (5): Luis Santos/Shutterstock; p. 29 (6): Rostislav Glinsky/Shutterstock; p. 29 (7): Songquan Deng/Shutterstock; p. 29 (8): Dutourdumonde Photography/Shutterstock; p. 29 (9): Kamira/Shutterstock; p. 29 (10): p. 30 (opener): Simon GRATIEN/Getty Images; Tupungato/Shutterstock; p. 30 (1L): Andrey Guryanov/Alamy; p. 30 (1M): Kinga/Shutterstock; p. 30 (1R): Tyler Olson/Shutterstock; p. 30 (2L): lightwavemedia/Shutterstock; p. 30 (2M): Monkey Business Images/Shutterstock; p. 30 (2R): FXQuadro/Shutterstock; p. 30 (3L): SergeBertasiusPhotography/Shutterstock; p. 30 (3M): Monkey Business Images/Shutterstock; p. 30 (3R): Andresr/Shutterstock; p. 30 (4L): Ollyy/Shutterstock; p. 30 (4M): Hero Images Inc./Alamy; p. 30 (4R): Byelikova Oksana/Shutterstock; p. 31 (1): Aaron Amat/Shutterstock; p. 31 (2): Monika Wisniewska/Shutterstock; p. 31 (3): Photographee.eu/Shutterstock; p. 31 (4): Pressmaster/Shutterstock; p. 33: fototrav/Getty Images; p. 35 (TL): Jiri Hera/Shutterstock; p. 35 (TM): Yulia Vybornyh/Shutterstock; p. 35 (TR): exopixel/Shutterstock; p. 35 (ML): Africa Studio/Shutterstock; p. 35 (MM): Mark Medcalf/Shutterstock; p. 35 (MR): Naypong/Shutterstock; p. 35

(BL): Bohbeh/Shutterstock; p. 35 (BM): Pitchayarat Chootai/Shutterstock; p. 35 (BR): Remember/Alamy; p. 36: Tom Bean/Alamy; p. 37 (1): Minerva Studio/Shutterstock; p. 37 (2): Dragon Images/Shutterstock; p. 37 (3): Elnur/Shutterstock; p. 37 (4): Andresr/Shutterstock; p. 37 (5): Hitdelight/Shutterstock; p. 37 (6): EDHAR/Shutterstock; p. 37 (7): bikeriderlondon/Shutterstock; p. 37 (8): Peter Bernik/Shutterstock; p. 37 (9): Monika Wisniewska/Shutterstock; p. 37 (10): Blend Images/Shutterstock; p. 37 (B): oneinchpunch/Shutterstock; p. 39 (TL): Elliot Hurwitt/Shutterstock; p. 39 (TM): Destinyweddingstudio/Shutterstock; p. 38: Thomas Marent/Minden Pictures/Corbis; p. 39 (TR): covenant/Shutterstock; p. 39 (BR): Tracy Starr/Shutterstock; p. 39 (BM): D. Kucharski K. Kucharska/Shutterstock; p. 39 (BR): Leena Robinson/Shutterstock; p. 41 (b/g): Subbotina Anna/Shutterstock; p. 41 (TR): AndreAnita/Shutterstock; p. 43 (a): Aleksey Stemmer/Shutterstock: p. 43 (b): O'SHI/Shutterstock; p. 43 (c): anekoho/Shutterstock; p. 43 (d): margouillat photo/Shutterstock; p. 43 (e): Denis Vesely/Shutterstock; p. 43 (f): Tracy Whiteside/Shutterstock; p. 44: Thomas Dressier/Getty Images; p. 45: f8grapher/Shutterstock; p. 48 (opener): Richard Rudisill/Getty Images; p. 48 (1): margouillat photo/Shutterstock; p. 48 (2): B. and E. Dudzinscy/Shutterstock; p. 48 (3): vsl/Shutterstock; p. 48 (4): marmo81/Shutterstock; p. 48 (5): qingqing/Shutterstock; p. 48 (6): bitt24/Shutterstock; p. 48 (7): ACORN 1/Alamy; p. 48 (8): Cefo design/Shutterstock; p. 48 (9): Elina Manninen/Shutterstock; p. 48 (10): Pixelspieler/Shutterstock; p. 49: Gelpi JM/Shutterstock; p. 50: Valua Vitaly/Shutterstock; p. 51: Marina Grau/Shutterstock; p. 53 (TL): imageBROKER/Alamy; p. 53 (TLC): Dynamicfoto/Shutterstock; p. 53 (TRC): Karel Gallas/Shutterstock; p. 53 (TR): Maksim Toome/Shutterstock; p. 53 (ML): nito/Shutterstock; p. 53 (MLC): Diego Cervo/Shutterstock; p. 53 (MRC): Yeko Photo Studio/Shutterstock; p. 53 (MR): Mr. Tobin/Shutterstock; p. 53 (BL): Ron van Elst/Shutterstock; p. 53 (BM): robert_s/Shutterstock; p. 53 (BR): KAMONRAT/Shutterstock; p. 54: Paul Souders/Corbis; p. 55 (TL): sdeva/Shutterstock; p. 55 (BR): Valentyn Volkov/Shutterstock; p. 56: Hero Images/Getty Images; p. 59: Irina Mos/Shutterstock; p. 61 (TL): PHILIPIMAGE/Shutterstock; p. 61 (TLC): Olgysha/Shutterstock; p. 61 (TC): samantha grandy/Shutterstock; p. 61 (TRC): Moving Moment/Shutterstock; p. 61 (TR): papkin/Shutterstock; p. 61 (BL): cristovao/Shutterstock; p. 61 (BLC): Andresr/Shutterstock; p. 61 (BC): Richard Thornton/Shutterstock; p. 61 (BRC): Moving Moment/Shutterstock; p. 61 (BR): Efired/Shutterstock; p. 62 (opener): Everything/Shutterstock; p. 62 (a): Mikhail Pozhenko/Shutterstock; p. 62 (b): aliasemma/Shutterstock; p. 62 (c): viki2win/Shutterstock; p. 62 (d): gemphoto/Shutterstock; p. 62 (e): Binkski/Shutterstock; p. 63: Julija Sapic/Shutterstock; p. 64 (TL): Amarita/Shutterstock; p. 64 (TC): bitt24/Shutterstock; p. 64 (TR): Yeko Photo Studio/Shutterstock; p. 64 (BL): Olga Miltsova/Shutterstock; p. 64 (BC): Anna Kurzaeva/Shutterstock; p. 64 (BR): travellight/Shutterstock; p. 66: Krzysztof Dydynski/Getty Images; p. 69: balabolka/Shutterstock; p. 72 (opener): Sasa Komien/Shutterstock; p. 72 (1): Elena Elisseeva/Shutterstock; p. 72 (a): david5962/Shutterstock; p. 72 (2): Givaga/Shutterstock; p. 72 (b): ronstik/Shutterstock; p. 72 (3): Mona Makela/Shutterstock; p. 72 (c): Rafal Cichawa/Shutterstock; p. 72 (4): Gromovataya/Shutterstock; p. 72 (d): Lukasz Pajor/Shutterstock; p. 72 (B): Cedric Weber/Shutterstock; p. 73: ilozavr/Shutterstock; p. 74 (opener): All Canada Photos/Alamy; p. 74 (1a): Rawpixel/Shutterstock; p. 74 (1b + 3b): Ase/Shutterstock; p. 74 (2a + 7a + 8a): Pakhnyushchy/Shutterstock; p. 74 (2b + 3a): behindlens/Shutterstock; p. 74 (4a): victorass/Shutterstock; p. 74 (4b + 5b + 6b): Artur Synenko/Shutterstock; p. 74 (5a): Christian Mueller/Shutterstock; p. 74 (7b): Gts/Shutterstock; p. 74 (B): Tomi/Shutterstock; p. 77 (b/g): nodff/Shutterstock; p. 77 (T): Jeff Williams/Alamy; p. 79 (TL): pisaphotography/Shutterstock; p. 79 (TLC): Robert Hoetink/Alamy; p. 79 (TRC): bikeriderlondon/Shutterstock; p. 79 (TR): Juice Images/Alamy; p. 79 (BL): alex2004/Shutterstock; p. 79 (BLC): Hung Chung Chih/Shutterstock; p. 79 (BRC): StudioSmart/Shutterstock; p. 79 (BR): Kiwisoul/Shutterstock; p. 80 (opener): Wan Ru Chen/Getty Images; p. 80 (a): Mihai Simonia/Shutterstock; p. 80 (b): Minerva Studio/Shutterstock; p. 80 (c): Vadym Zaitsev/Shutterstock; p. 80 (d): B747/Shutterstock; p. 80 (e): Igumnova Irina/Shutterstock; p. 81: Enigma/Alamy; p. 93: StepanPopov/Shutterstock.

Front cover photo by Gerardo Ricardo Lopez/Getty Images